DIGITAL DIVIDE IN POST-COVID-19 ERA

Hiram Herrera Rivas

Cd. Victoria, Tamaulipas, México

November 2024

CONTENT

INDEX OF FIGURES

INDEX OF TABLES

Dedication:

This book is dedicated to my family

Acknowledgements:

I thank all the teachers who have shared their valuable knowledge
with me through formal and non-formal education.

Introduction

Today, lifelong learning is increasingly shaped by information technology, which can enhance cognitive skills when used effectively. While access to computers and the Internet is believed to improve educational outcomes, it does not address underlying structural inequalities in society. The rise of information and communication technologies has raised expectations for an equitable distribution of knowledge, but disparities persist, reinforcing existing cultural gaps rather than resolving them. The ongoing scientific and technological revolution has further widened this gap, and with recent advances in robotics and artificial intelligence tools, the gap continues to evolve in new ways, such as the "robotics gap," which is the natural evolution of the digital divide; it is worth mentioning that industries demand an increasingly skilled workforce so that people can have a well-paid job. Furthermore, in 2020, the COVID-19 pandemic exacerbated existing educational disparities around the world by forcing a rapid transition to online learning, leaving many teachers and students unprepared for this change. This paper aims to review all the concepts and stakeholders involved in the digital divide and its evolution over time.

Keywords: Digital divide; Digital literacy; Knowledge society, Covid 19.

The government's approach to the digital divide

In Mexico, the government sector is once again taking part in telecommunications; the example was the rescue of Altán Networks by the government sector; the above would help bring internet access to more rural areas of Mexico. The president's promise was to bring internet to all communities in Mexico and he stated that this firm can cover 70% of the country on its own. To encourage development, the president said that it is crucial to connect the nation. Through the new Mexican State corporation, internet access will be available in all communities in the country, accessing information and educational materials available online. This action responds to the fact that currently internet service providers focus on providing internet in large urban areas, where people have more purchasing power, creating a digital divide in rural areas (AMLO, 2022) . Consequently, Mexico can adapt to the evolution of information and communication technologies. The adoption of these technologies can bring important advantages to society. It is said that whenever a new technology appears, such as information and communication technologies, it is assumed that it has great potential and can help us solve the underlying problems of society. The reality is that in general the appearance of new technologies makes social divisions even worse. Therefore, it is essential that citizens of the 21st century adopt a proactive position and face these new technological changes for the benefit of society in general, trying to "soften" their negative impacts and overcome the digital divide, which is a multiform gap, including differences in gender, age, educational level, language, infrastructure and use. Digital literacy is no longer just a topic for IT and telecommunications specialists, but has become a basic and transversal competence for people.

Current Internet adoption rates in Mexico

The Mexican Institute of Statistics and Geography states that 78% of people (88.5 million) in Mexico's urban cities were internet users in 2021, however, the region with the most connectivity in the country is Mexico City with 88% of people connected, and the least connected region in the country is the state of Chiapas, on the southern border with Central America there are 46% of people who use the internet. It is vital to note that indigenous people make up around 28% of the population in Chiapas, which may contribute to the racial digital divide. It is notable to see that 96% of people use smartphones as their primary means of accessing the internet. The next most popular internet access devices are laptops, which are used by 27% of people. Their adoption rate is almost as high as that of smart TVs, which are used by 25% of people. Other devices that are less popular for connecting to the Internet are desktop computers, which are used by 15% of people, followed by tablets, which are used by 9.7% of people, and finally, video game consoles, which are used by 6.5% of people (INEGI, 2021) .

Table 1. Home Internet without a telephone package in Mexico.

Internet Service Provider	Speed (Mbps)	Cost (USD)
BLUE TELECOMMUNICATIONS	5	$13
DARLING	5	$13
TVE	5	$13
DISH	5	$13.25
BAIT	5	$13.25
TELMEX	5	$17
IZZI	10	$17
Telcel	10	$19.55
MOVISTAR	12	$19.55
AT&T	10	$22

Source: (SELECTRA, 2022) .

The increasing availability of mobile and fixed broadband has a positive effect on the economic growth of Latin America, a study used data from 20 countries from 2010-2018 and created a simultaneous equation model; the results showed a positive contribution to the economic growth of the region (Alderete, 2022) .

Learning and the information society

Learning is a continuous process in human beings, which occurs from childhood, continues into youth and transcends into adulthood. Education is a complex process in which an expert tutor and an apprentice interact; in the learning process a binomial is formed: expert-apprentice. In this process, learning tools and objects can interact; a current tool for learning is information technology. However, as with all learning tools, the usefulness of the computer with an Internet connection will have a positive effect on the development of cognitive skills only when it is supported by its correct use as a learning tool. Today's university is immersed in the information society; new generations of students enter the University immersed in it. The use of a computer with an Internet connection at home should be a factor supporting education that helps to increase the student's cognitive bases. It is often assumed that technology will radically end inequality and solve by itself the structural problems of people's daily lives. With the advent of information and communication technologies came the hope that knowledge would be accessible to all, however, knowledge has not reached everyone equally (Correa-Gutiérrez et al., 2015) . New media often inspire hope that they can and will be used to address cultural divides. This hope is projected onto new technologies in ways that suggest that the technology itself will do the work of resolving cultural divides. The existence of a new technology does not create or solve cultural problems, in fact its construction often reinforces existing social divides (Deogracias, 2015) . It may be wrongly assumed that access to a computer and an Internet connection will significantly improve our standard of living. In order to acquire new skills and stimulate our levels of thinking, for example our logical-mathematical intelligence or our linguistic intelligence, it is necessary to develop skills that help us better understand cultural differences. It is not enough to have a computer with an Internet connection. It is necessary to carry out a correct strategy of tutoring and digital literacy by experts in the field with the appropriate exercises and specialized software that helps us raise the level of cognitive skills, whatever they may be. The dissemination of knowledge through teaching and the generation of new knowledge through scientific research are functions of today's university. In addition, the university also has the function of extension, whose purpose has to do with its influence on life in society. The results of the influence of the university on society can be classified as social, economic and political. The greatest challenge that society faces together with the university, since it is immersed in it, is inequality (Luna-Pla et al., 2015) ; in the information age, inequality manifests itself as the Digital Divide.

Digital divide

The issue of the Digital Divide, or as its name in English "Digital Divide" has evolved over time, giving rise to new definitions and concepts, such as the concept of "Digital Literacy" and the concept of "Digital Inclusion". Here we will build the main definitions with which we will work from now on. The digital divide is a condition of human underdevelopment where cultural and social aspects transcend the technological (Luna-Pla et al., 2015) . We can visualize the above in this way: With the current advances in computing and the Internet, human beings require new transversal skills, just as reading and writing were before, now knowledge of the tools of the digital age is required, such as the use of the computer and the consultation of information on the Internet, as well as the use of the Internet as a new learning tool, supported by online courses and tutorials, which can take us to a new level of cognitive development. Different authors express their definitions on the evolution of the Digital Divide, including access, use and quality of use (Fernández, 2005) . In the life cycle of the Internet with respect to users (figure 1) we can see that initially there are people who have the opportunity to access technology and other people who do not have the opportunity to access it. This first inequality between individuals is known as the digital access gap. In a second moment, technology begins to satisfy basic needs and the technology adoption curve rises, increasing the number of users of said technology as time goes by. In a second moment in time, there are divisions of technology users according to their use. For example, there may be users who use computer technology to improve the learning of a second language, as opposed to other users who use this technology for fun and entertainment, such as video games or social networks. In a third moment, at the stage of technology saturation, at this moment the technology has reached the peak of users in a population, here we can observe the differences in the quality of use of the technology by the users.

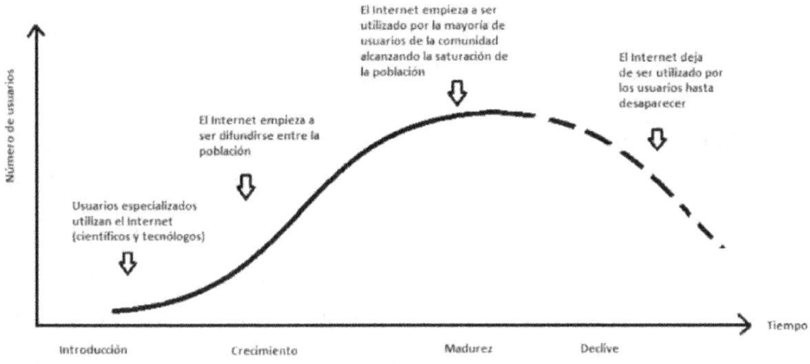

Figure 1. Internet adoption by users and its life cycle (Own elaboration).

The digital divide is studied as a phenomenon that occurs in different parts of the world. In North America, particularly in the United States, researchers conduct an analysis of the Digital Divide (Straubhaar, 2012) and new concepts were constructed, based on the theoretical model of Bourdieu's Habitus, which helped to better understand the phenomenon of the Digital Divide. These concepts mention cultural capital, economic capital and social capital, which are adapted to the context of a technological society; some of these concepts are:

- ➢ Techno-field: It is the professional area of a person regarding technology.
- ➢ Techno-capital: It is the knowledge and skills that a person has regarding computers.
- ➢ Technology readiness: Individuals' attitudes toward computers and technology; described by indicators such as social practices, perceptions, attitudes, technical education, desire for information, job requirements, community interactions, and geographic location.

Straubhaar locates his study in Austin, Texas, which was emerging as a new technopolis in the 21st century. It is mentioned that Austin's emergence as a technopolis radically influences the economy and education of its inhabitants, as well as the necessary skills required to adapt to a knowledge city; it is also mentioned that technological skills, readiness for technology and access to technologies are very important in a technopolis, and it is mentioned that in the United States the educational level of people has been directly related to obtaining better jobs. For example, we can mention the particular case of Information Technology, where to obtain a good job, in addition to obtaining a university degree, it is desirable for companies that a candidate also have a "certification" that validates their digital skills in a particular technology. An example is the Computing Technology Industry Association, a non-profit organization founded in 1982 dedicated to certifying professional competencies for the information technology industry. In the United States, a company may require a candidate applying for a new job to have an A+ certification issued by CompTIA, which focuses on hardware and software skills for the maintenance and repair of computer equipment, in order to fill a required vacancy. This industry certification culture is permeating other countries given the cultural influence of American companies. On the other hand, we have Mexico, where a certain company may require the same A+ certification issued by CompTIA in order to fill a job position in Mexico. Although there are certification centers in Mexico where a candidate can take their A+ certification exam, a Mexican candidate has a double gap to overcome, since certification exams are often available in English and not available in Spanish. This situation can occur in several countries around the world, where a technology skills certification exam is not available in the candidate's native language.

Multiplicity of forms of the digital divide

The digital divide is a multiform divide (Cruz-Capote, 2022) that is made up of many other divides. Below are some of the factors that make it up:

Education: The evolution of the "post-industrial" society will require considerable investments in education and training (Zapata-Ros, 2013) ; it is at this point where a close relationship is established between knowledge societies and the information society. If people are not trained, they would not be able to obtain benefits even if they had access to computing infrastructure and Internet connection (Correa-Gutiérrez et al., 2015) ; it mentions that the educational and social problem called the digital divide is a form of exclusion that has increased the separation between regions and countries, which is why it is called the international digital divide; it also mentions that the existing separation between citizens of the same society is called the domestic digital divide; something of primary concern is also mentioned that can be seen as the cognitive gap that separates the most favored countries from developing countries and more specifically from the less developed countries, presenting a constant risk that this gap will increase. The above is valid for both gaps. The cognitive gap is related to the educational level of the user. One of the cognitive abilities of a person is the ability to convert information into knowledge (Correa-Gutiérrez et al., 2015) . Theoretically, the higher the educational level and the level of knowledge a user has, the more benefit he or she can obtain from the information available on the Internet; we can also affirm that if a user has a low educational level and knowledge, he or she will be able to obtain little benefit from the Internet.

This work takes into account the educational level of the student entering higher education, which is assumed to have been formed mainly in the schools he/she attended in his/her basic and upper secondary education before applying for admission to higher education, as well as in his/her family environment.

Language: Although globalization forces us to use the new lingua franca, as Latin was once, we are now faced with the predominance of the English language, which remains the dominant lingua franca until 2017. The largest number of nodes and domains on the Internet belong to the United States and other English-speaking countries (Correa-Gutiérrez et al., 2015) . This presents a gap between different peoples and societies that do not have access to mastery of this language, limiting them from entering the new era of education and the global economy; we can mention that this gap is accentuated for indigenous peoples on all continents, where there are social groups whose majority of members still use an indigenous language.

Age: Age is a determining factor in every society, because in each of our societies, regardless of their location Geographically, there will always be a generation gap that is continuous and lasts over time.

Gender: Governments and institutions must promote women's access, participation and success at all levels of education (Cruz-Capote, 2022) . In developing countries, there is a risk that women accumulate a series of disadvantages that prevent them from accessing new technologies as well as education. A gender equity policy will ensure that an equal number of men and women have access to higher education.

Access: We can mention that we are currently in a transition from information societies to knowledge societies. The information society is presented to us as a global society hyperconnected through public and private networks and the Internet, which includes access to various information systems through different computing devices; it is possible to measure the speed with which an Internet connection is made, as well as the number of personal computers, laptops and mobile devices that one has; the availability of connecting to the Internet at work and at home; we can also mention access to various public information systems as well as access to exclusive or paid private databases; until 2018, not all information on the Internet is available for public use or is freely accessible, as there are some paid databases.

Use: The use given to the information available on the Internet is as important as the knowledge itself; one would think that the Internet is a great tool for education, in itself it is, but it can also be a great distraction and cause a great waste of time, since it can trap the minds of users among the large amount of content available for leisure such as video games, social networks, pages and entertainment websites; we can see the above as the "time thieves", which can be social networks (Facebook, Twitter, WhatsApp) as well as video games and consoles capable of connecting to play collaboratively on the Internet. We can also mention the existence of Smart TVs, with a large amount and availability of digital content for leisure. In a study it was established that students who lived in a regime with few parental restrictions used the computer more frequently for recreational or playful purposes (Ahn & Vigdor, 2014) ; It was also mentioned that parental restrictions, in turn, may be less strict in single-parent households or in households where both parents work outside the home. This introduces the possibility that computer technology in the home may have negative effects on the academic performance of some students.

Knowledge societies

Mention will be made of the existence of ***digital solidarity,*** that is, the creation of a more just and collaborative society on the Internet, where work groups are formed that are geographically dispersed but digitally united with a common interest or goal. It is said that freedom ***of expression is the cornerstone of knowledge societies;*** the fact that freedom of expression is guaranteed in a government and in a society will lead us, at least in theory, to a more just democratic society where human rights are respected.

Learning societies ; education is no longer the privilege of an elite and is no longer linked to a certain age; it tends to extend both to the entire community and to the duration of an individual's existence (UNESCO, 2005) ; education and learning are not limited only to school environments, but also exist in non-formal education, as well as in continuous learning in organizations.

A culture of innovation; "...currently, culture itself is built based more on the model of creativity and renewal than on the model of permanence and reproduction; the generalization of learning at all levels of society should be the logical counterpart of the permanent instability created by the culture of innovation..." (UNESCO, 2005) ; the above is visible in a capitalist society, where the entry of innovative products and processes give a clear competitive advantage to the companies and organizations that adopt them; it would be worth asking ourselves at this point, who are the actors that generate most of the innovations in society, that is, the current economy is based on innovation, but could it be that the vast majority of members of society produce a large number of innovations? We would have to define a generalized quantitative way of measuring the level of innovation generated by each individual.

Learning to learn is a key value in knowledge societies. This is evident because the amount of knowledge available today and the speed at which it is generated is enormous. Given the above, it is clear that the ability to learn by oneself is of great importance in today's era.

Availability of knowledge; it is desirable that all of humanity's knowledge be public, however, although a large amount of knowledge is in the public domain, there are still digital contents that are exclusive or pay-per-use. It is said that there are currently two monopolies of knowledge: educational institutions and books; it is also mentioned that the appearance of the Internet will greatly affect the two aforementioned monopolies of knowledge. Two important concepts about the generated texts are ubiquity (availability anywhere) and fluidity (that the texts can be easily commented, discussed and modified).

Basic education for all; education is a right universally proclaimed in the Universal Declaration of Human Rights (1948):

> ➤ Everyone has the right to education. Education shall be free, at least as regards elementary and fundamental education. Elementary education shall be compulsory. Technical and vocational education shall be general. Access to higher education shall be equal for all, according to their respective merits.

> ➤ Education shall aim at the full development of the human personality and at strengthening respect for human rights and fundamental freedoms; it shall promote understanding, tolerance and friendship among nations and all ethnic and religious groups; and it shall promote the development of United Nations peacekeeping activities. Therefore, we can affirm that basic education must also contemplate digital access and skills for all.

E-education: Distance education; distance education emerges as a new alternative to meet the demand for education in geographically distant places.

Higher education market, financing issue; in recent decades, great importance has been given to higher education, which has led to its massification; however, university education represents a significant cost, which must be covered, either by the government or by individuals. An alternative for higher education is its financing, which will allow access to education for a greater number of students.

University networks to be invented; it is said that, with globalization and the great specialization of knowledge today, it is very difficult and inefficient to concentrate experts in a discipline of knowledge and research in a single institution and a single geographic space; given the above, it is necessary to create new university networks of experts in various lines of knowledge to articulate the new generation of knowledge.

New missions of higher education According to the 1998 World Conference on Higher Education, the main functions of higher education institutions are:

Monitor, alert and analyse the most important problems of society; adapt to the needs of the world of work, without losing one's own identity and submitting to it; analyse the other levels of the educational system to generate a project for society; build a culture in society, because culture is not something that is given, but is built in space and time, taking into account different cultures; increase the participation of disadvantaged groups, especially women; promote lifelong education, that is, education throughout life, through flexible and appropriate strategies; promote the active participation of students in research, teaching, management and the life of institutions.

New research centres, the vocation for science is universal, but scientific advances seem to be exclusive to one part of the planet. Kofi Annan, former Secretary General of the United Nations, said: "The idea that there can be two worlds of science is anathema to the scientific spirit." Research systems must be created that are based on the quadruple helix model: Government, Business, University and

Society, adapting the above to the situation of each country to the extent of its political, economic and academic capacities. International scientific collaboration must be guided by four fundamental principles, according to Roger Pedersen in 2003:

*Techniques and materials must be standardized as much as possible so that results can be accurately compared and reproduced; a co-laboratory is a decentralized system that can only function if the institutions that comprise it work in harmony (notion of interoperability).

*Research work should be complementary; the division of labor between laboratories makes it possible to avoid duplication of tasks.

*Technologies that allow greater efficiency and speed should be used.

*For a research program to serve the common good, a balance must be found between the dissemination, validation and review of data and the determination and protection of intellectual property.

New frontiers of science, it is said that the evidence of the knowledge society are the advances in transdisciplinary sciences such as biology, nanotechnology and computer science. It is known that from now on it will be necessary to take research in computer science much further, if only to address phenomena as important for global governance as climate change or the evolution of financial markets. These objects, called "complex adaptive systems", require immense computing capacities because they comprise a multiplicity of variables that need to be studied globally. The study of "Info-nanobiotechnology" should be encouraged, machines that work at a molecular level, for medical purposes and food production; the man-machine interface should be improved, that is, connecting the nervous system of a living organism with automata.

Crisis in science education, scientific culture, according to UNESCO there is a crisis in science education, especially in developing countries, that is why it is important to promote the teaching of science and technology in less developed countries and that these are not a privilege exclusive to first world countries.

Cognitive gap, it is said that this type of gap is the most critical, which tends to increase even with the advances in current science and technology, due to inequality in resources.

Economic, scientific and cultural aspects in first world countries and in developing countries, as well as within the same country, between different social strata. The idea is to apply digital inclusion to all strata of society.

Digital literacy

Each country in the world has the responsibility to grow the human capital of its citizens; this objective is met by completing the years of basic education of each person, but it is also important to have a method of continuing education throughout life, due to the dynamic change of the labor market; In addition, companies have the need for a trained human workforce with skills according to their specific needs. A relevant part of education to have a trained workforce are digital skills because if a person has good digital skills, they could improve all their other person skills, this is achieved thanks to the availability of hundreds of online courses that exist today. In Mexico, there is a digital platform with hundreds of free online courses for digital literacy, the platform is called "aprende.org" which means "learn" (Slim, 2022) ; the platform has digital content sections such as the National Biodiversity Pavilion, the Soumaya Museum, Culture and Education, Training for employment, and Health. In addition, "aprpende.org" has links to redirect to other important digital platforms from other countries such as Academica, Khan Academy, Coursera, Udacity and Massachusetts Institute of Technology Open Courseware; the Aprende.org platform is sponsored by the Carlos Slim Foundation in an effort to unite the private sector, government, academic institutions and civil society so that its education, employment, health, economic and social development, migrants, sports, environment, culture, and human development programs help a large sector of Latin American society with a focus on the most vulnerable groups.

UNESCO: Approaches to the application of information technologies in education

There are studies on the application of Information Technologies in developed and developing countries that allow to identify at least four major approaches through which educational systems and schools proceed to the adoption and use of ICT (Unesco, 2002) . Although these approaches were visualized by UNESCO and reported in 2002, several years later in 2024, it can be observed that these approaches are still valid and are applied in different parts of the world to educational systems and schools at all levels; the four different approaches of Information Technologies applied to education according to UNESCO are:

Emerge -> Apply -> Infuse -> Transform

Emerging approach

...In the emerging approach, schools or educational institutions can be considered as being at an early stage of development. In these educational centres, computer equipment and software are purchased or donated. In this initial phase, educators and administrators explore the possibilities and consequences of using ICTs in school management and their integration into the academic part to promote learning. However, teaching practices are rooted in traditional teacher-centred practice. Awareness of the use of Information Technologies to support learning is generated in the teaching and student community; this is important in order to move on to the next approach... (Unesco, 2002) .

The application approach

...In these schools and education systems, the contribution of information technologies to learning is better understood. In this second phase, administrators and teachers use ICTs for tasks already performed in school management and in the curriculum. Teachers largely dominate the learning environment. Schools in the implementation or focus phase adapt the curriculum to increase the use of ICTs in various subject areas with specific tools and software. This curriculum supports the move to the next focus if desired... (Unesco, 2002) .

The infusion approach

...In the next stage, the infusion approach involves the integration or incorporation of ICTs throughout the curriculum, and is seen in schools that now employ a variety of technologies in computer labs, classrooms and administrative offices. Teachers explore new ways of adapting IT to their personal productivity and professional practice. The curriculum begins to merge subject areas to reflect real-world applications... (Unesco, 2002) .

The transformative approach

...Schools and educational systems that use information technology to creatively rethink and renew school organization are at the stage of a transformative approach. Information technology becomes an integral and invisible part of daily personal productivity and professional practice. The curriculum is learner-centred, integrating subject areas into real-world applications. Information technology is taught as a separate subject at the vocational level and is incorporated into all vocational areas. Schools have become true learning centres for their communities... (Unesco, 2002) . The various approaches to the adoption of ICT in learning have already been reviewed, now it is important to mention the model of the teaching-learning stages that a person goes through when learning to use a new digital tool; there are four moments that the human being experiences in his journey through the digital world and his learning. These stages are the discovery of the digital tool, learning the digital tool, understanding when and how to use the digital tool and finally specializing in the use of a certain digital tool (see figure 2). Digital tools can be considered as Information and Communication Technology tools, abbreviated as ICT tools. It is said that the good use of ICT tools will lead us to correct digital literacy; Table 1 shows an example of modules and units of the ICT curriculum for secondary school modified and adapted by Herrera-Rivas for the year 2024.

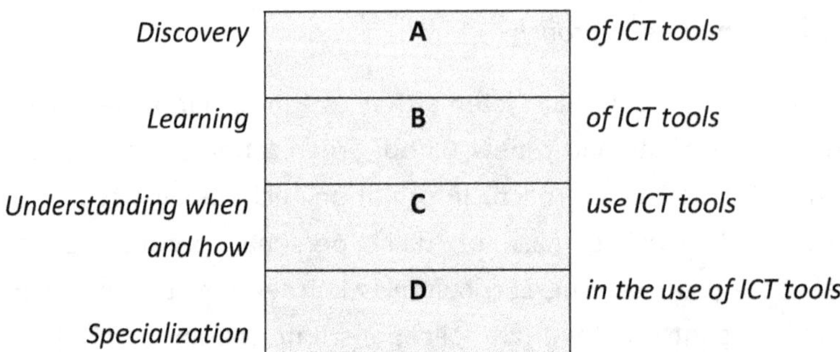

Figure 2. Model of teaching-learning stages with and through Information and Communication Technologies (Unesco, 2002) .

Literacy Digital	Application of ICT in subjects	Incorporating ICT into the curriculum	Specialization in ICT
Units	Units	Units	Units
Fundamentals of ICT	Languages and ICT	Reading promotion	Introduction to programming
Computer use and file management	ICT and natural sciences	Are we being genetically modified?	Object Oriented Programming
Word processor	ICT in mathematics	Antarctica 2100	Software engineering
Spreadsheet	ICT in social sciences	Multimedia tools	
Presentation design	ICT in art	1920 and its excesses	Mobile Device Programming
Database management	Measurement	Problems of society	Computer vision
Information and communication	Modeling and simulation	Effects of globalization	Management information systems
Social and ethical aspects	Robots and feedback elements	3D CAD Design	Systems and process control
The world of work with ICT	Statistics		Project management
	Music		
Artificial Intelligence Tools for Human Assistance	Database design		Data mining
	Spreadsheet design		IPv6 and the Internet of Things

Figure 3. Example of modules and units from the UNESCO ICT curriculum for secondary schools (2002), modified and adapted by Herrera-Rivas for 2024.

OECD: Digital skills for the 21st century

The OECD's position has been developed through two major initiatives: The Definition and Selection of Competencies (DeSeCo) and the Programme for International Student Assessment (PISA), launched in 1997. The first of these aimed to provide a framework that could guide the long-term development of assessments of these new competences, grouping the key competences into three groups: a) Interactive use of tools; b) Interaction between heterogeneous groups; c) Acting autonomously; the ability of individuals to think for themselves and take responsibility for their learning and actions lies at the heart of this framework. The results of DeSeCo form the theoretical basis of PISA, which seeks to monitor the extent to which students at the limit of compulsory education (15 years) have acquired the knowledge and skills necessary to participate fully in society. It focuses on the ability of young people to use their knowledge and skills in relation to real-life challenges, rather than on their ability to master a specific school curriculum. Taking into account the OECD position, skills and competencies can be grouped into the following categories:

*Functional ICT skills, including relevant skills for the proper use of different applications.

*ICT skills for learning, which include skills that combine cognitive and higher-order activities with functional skills for the use and management of these applications.

*21st century skills, necessary for the knowledge society where the use of ICT is not a necessary condition.

Definition of competence:

… "A competence is more than knowledge or skills, it involves the ability to meet complex demands by drawing on and mobilizing psychosocial resources (including skills and attitudes) in a particular context; for example, the ability to communicate effectively is a competence that can represent a person's knowledge of a language, practical skills, and attitudes toward those with whom he or she communicates." … (Rychen & Salganik, 2003) .

Below is a theoretical framework that conceptualizes the competencies discussed above, which can be taught according to three dimensions: information, communication, and ethical-social impact.

Information dimension

a) Information as a source: Search, selection, evaluation and organization of information;

b) Information as a product, the restructuring and modelling of information and the development of one's own ideas (knowledge).

Dimension of communication

a) Effective communication, processing, transformation and formatting of information, as well as reflection on the best way to present an idea to a given audience.

b) Virtual collaboration and interaction: ICTs provide tools for collaborative work between peers inside and outside school, through the spontaneous creation of learning communities; participation in digital culture depends on the ability to interact within groups of virtual friends or groups that share the same interest.

Ethical dimension and social impact

a) Social responsibility, in relation to ICTs, refers to the ability to apply criteria for their responsible use both at a personal and social level, recognizing potential risks, as well as the use of standards of behavior that promote appropriate social exchange through the network. Critical thinking, responsibility and decision-making are competencies of this subdivision.

b) Social impact: This dimension refers to the development of an awareness of the challenges of the new digital era. For example, there is consensus that young people should reflect on the great impact of ICTs on social life, considering the social, economic and cultural implications for the individual and society.

Analysis of UNESCO's discourse towards the OECD

The OECD proposes to train individuals with skills and abilities for the 21st century in the digital era and economy. Individuals must have certain skills and abilities to be able to function in the economic sphere, find employment and be useful to society. UNESCO, on the other hand, is concerned about the divisions that the digital divide will create, namely the gender gap, the language gap, the cognitive gap, the economic gap. It focuses on the Universal Declaration of Human Rights, which states that everyone has the right to education. It proposes new functions for universities, which are to look after society. It also proposes that new university networks be invented, where there are communities of scientific and technological development. UNESCO proposes that science and technology should not be a privilege of the first world, but should also be encouraged in less developed countries. UNESCO has also explored the development of an Information Technology curriculum, which defines everything from basic computer skills to specialized computer skills that can be taught in secondary education. The development of computer skills coincides with the development of skills proposed by the OECD, which focuses on the skills to generate new knowledge from existing knowledge, focusing on the individual's higher order skills, in addition to promoting the individual's communication capacity, as well as online collaboration, and also emphasizing an ethical dimension and the social impact of knowledge (Kinnari & Silvennoinen, 2023) .

Digital natives, digital migrants and digital wisdom

The generation gap that currently exists in all societies around the world is once again manifested in its digital component. Prensky first mentioned an analysis between digital natives and digital migrants in 2001. Another contribution by Prensky is the concept of "digital wisdom" which postulates that computers and the Internet act as an extension of the human mind, providing an increase in its memory capacity and information processing. Prensky's theory of digital natives is based on two fundamental premises:

1. The young generation of digital natives possesses sophisticated knowledge and skills in information technologies.

2. As a result of their education and technology, digital natives have particular learning preferences that are different from previous generations of students.

The Digital Natives theory puts emphasis on the digital skills of the Natives and their learning style. It is not clear how the new digital technology will affect the different types of thinking that are assessed in academic life, such as logical-mathematical thinking and linguistic-verbal thinking; it is suggested that these types of thinking be stimulated by this new technology; for this, an adequate digital literacy ecosystem must be in place, with specialized software to stimulate each type of thinking, as well as the appropriate tutoring strategies and an expert tutor (Spiegel, 2021) .

Prensky presents us with a generational society, divided by those who were born in the digital age vs those who were caught up with the digital age in adulthood. This theory of digital natives has advanced since the term was first coined in 2001. In its most recent version, we are presented with the concept of digital homo sapiens, as well as digital wisdom; digital homo sapiens, whether native or migrant, is a being adapted to the digital age where he uses digital computers, smartphones and the Internet as an extension of the human brain, where digital homo sapiens takes advantage of all the advantages of having access to instant information, artificial intelligence tools, Internet search tools, assistance for driving cars with GPS, collaborative learning with groups on social networks, assisted learning with videos on the Internet, unlike traditional homo sapiens who learned only from person to person and from books. Computers and the Internet complement some cognitive functions of the brain, making them more efficient. However, the large amount of information becomes a challenge, so a new skill is also required to process it; computer technology has surpassed the human mind in terms of memory capacity, access and search for information; the human mind has not been able to evolve as quickly to these changes, still needing certain learning in the traditional way; we still need human beings who are experts in the various areas of knowledge.

It is still necessary, but the huge amount of online content enables contact with experts and communities of experts virtually, online, asynchronously and remotely, placing all of humanity in one large global community or village.

COVID-19 setbacks

The digital divide existed before 2020 in many countries around the world, and many efforts have been made by governments, private initiatives and non-profit organizations to reduce the digital divide between society around the world. In fact, one objective of the 2030 Agenda for Asia-Pacific Economic Cooperation is to guarantee inclusive, equitable and quality education, and promote lifelong learning opportunities for all, and with this, face the challenge of unemployment posed by technological advances focused on automation (Girón et al., 2022) . In addition, the effects of the scientific and technological revolution are global, and affect various facets of social life; companies increasingly need innovation and automation, this context creates a new technological gap that ranges from the digital gap to the robotics gap (López-Peláez, 2014) . In addition to all the demands of society in terms of qualified labor to compete in 2021 in a digitalized and robotized economy, during 2020, the COVID-19 pandemic caused and will continue to cause an increase in unemployment, mainly attributable to the contraction of the economy and global production, the decrease in trade in goods and services, temporary job losses and the reduction in working hours caused by confinement, as well as bankrupt companies (Girón-Palau et al., 2020) .

The pandemic affected the economy and education, an example can be seen in Mexico where the head of the Ministry of Education expressed the failure to make the transition from traditional education to a more modern one with technology during the 2020 pandemic, as the Mexican government ordered educational institutions to cancel face-to-face classes, moving to online classes, remote classes by television and radio. Although distance courses and online courses were mature before the pandemic, most teachers and students throughout Mexico were not prepared for the change from face-to-face education to online and distance education; In addition, there was a difference between social sectors, younger K-12 students who had fewer social conditions were more vulnerable to greater poverty in every sense, both in the family itself and in technological resources, because they did not have computers. These students did not have the possibility of isolating themselves in a space to be able to have an online class, a virtual class in basic education (Ruiz-Gutierrez, 2024) .

Researchers from the Polytechnic University of Victoria (Mexico) interviewed university students to explore their feelings about the effects of Covid-19 (García-Juarez et al., 2024) the results are described below:

Expenses: Several students shared experiences that highlighted the significant reduction in transportation and food expenses when participating in online classes. This finding underscores a notable change in student spending patterns due to the transition to distance education.

Coexistence: Sharing the experience with classmates and teachers during online classes. These experiences covered a wide range of perceptions and emotions, reflecting the complexity of adapting to a virtual educational environment.

Performance: Diverse experiences were evident among students regarding their academic and personal performance when taking online classes. Some students expressed that the online class modality gave them greater flexibility in terms of time management and study structure. They highlighted that the possibility of accessing online learning materials at any time allowed them to adapt their study schedule to their individual preferences, which translated into an improvement in their academic performance by being able to better manage their time and delve deeper into the topics they found most challenging. In addition, some students mentioned that the online learning environment gave them greater autonomy and responsibility in their learning process, allowing them to develop self-discipline and self-management skills that they considered beneficial both for their academic performance and for their personal development.

Conclusions

Digital inequalities persist in affluent North American countries, revealing a stark contrast between technological advancement and access to it. Despite being at the forefront of digital innovation, significant segments of the population remain disconnected, perpetuating systemic inequalities. This phenomenon, often referred to as the digital divide, underscores the disparity in access to high-speed Internet and digital devices, particularly among low-income households and rural communities. Key implications discussed were:

Economic: Lack of reliable internet access severely limits economic opportunities for marginalized groups. Many people are unable to participate in the digital economy, which increasingly relies on technology for job applications and remote work. As a result, those without access face greater barriers to employment and income mobility.

Education: The educational landscape has been dramatically impacted by these inequalities, especially during the COVID-19 pandemic. Students from disadvantaged backgrounds struggled to engage in online learning due to insufficient access to technology and the internet. This "homework gap" has long-term implications for academic performance and future opportunities.

Social stratification: Digital inequalities also exacerbate social stratification. Communities with limited digital infrastructure often suffer isolation from broader societal developments, leading to a cycle of disadvantage that is difficult to break. The implications were profound: without targeted interventions, these disparities will continue to entrench existing inequalities between generations.

Finally, addressing these enduring digital inequalities is not simply a technological challenge but a fundamental societal imperative that requires comprehensive policy action and community engagement.

References

Ahn, T., & Vigdor, J. (2014). *The impact of No Child Left Behind's accountability sanctions on school performance: Regression discontinuity evidence from North Carolina* .

Alderete, MV (2022). The effect of broadband on economic growth in Latin America: an approach based on a simultaneous equations model.

AMLO. (2022). *Purchase of Altán Networks will contribute to bringing the internet to remote communities in the country* . Lopez Obrador. Retrieved 09/22/2024 from https://lopezobrador.org.mx/2022/06/13/compra-de-altan-redes-contribuira-a-llevar-internet-hasta-comunidades-alejadas-del-pais-presidente/

Correa-Gutiérrez, S., Balderas, E.R., García, H.M.C., & Sucedo, M.A.R. (2015). *Digital gaps in Tamaulipas and the basic education system* . Pearson. https://books.google.com.mx/books?id=5t1bzgEACAAJ

Cruz-Capote, M. (2022). Digital gaps and information and communications technologies (ICTs) in young people in Havana. *Novedades en Población Journal* , *18* (35), 244-275.

Deogracias, A. (2015). Danah Boyd: It's Complicated: The Social Lives of Networked Teens: Yale University Press, New Haven, Connecticut, 2014, pp. 296, ISBN 973-0-300-16631-6. In: Springer.

Fernández, FJ (2005). Digital divide and digital inclusion in Chile: the challenges of a new literacy. *Communicate* , *12* (24), 77-84. https://www.revistacomunicar.com/ojs/index.php/comunicar/article/view/C24-2005-12

García-Juarez, L., Herrera-Rivas, H., Hernández-Almazán, J.-A., Machucho-Cadena, R., & López-Luna, J.F. (2024). Exploring students' feelings about online classes during the COVID-19 pandemic. In RSQ (Ed.), *Research in education. Possibilities, tensions and challenges* (Vol. 1). Religación Press. https://doi.org/https://doi.org/10.46652/religacionpress.175.c173

Girón-Palau, J., Beltrán, D., & Castro, I. (2020). *Education and pandemic, an academic perspective* . UNAM. https://www.iisue.unam.mx/investigacion/textos/educacion_pandemia.pdf

Girón, A., Ivanova, A., & Zamora, A. (2022). *Mexico in APEC: Agenda in Times of Pandemic* . Bubok Publishing. https://www.bubok.com.mx/libros/268308/mexico-en-apec-agenda-en-tiempos-de-pandemia

INEGI. (2021). *National Survey on Availability and Use of Information Technologies in Households 2021* . INEGI. Retrieved 09/22/2024 from https://www.inegi.org.mx/programas/dutih/2021/

Kinnari, H., & Silvennoinen, H. (2023). Subjectivities of the lifelong learner in 'humanistic generation'-Critical policy analysis of lifelong learning policies among discourses of UNESCO, the Council of Europe and the OECD. *International Journal of Lifelong Education* , *42* (4), 424-440.

López-Peláez, A. (2014). *The Robotics Divide. A New Frontier in the 21st Century?* SpringerLondon. https://doi.org/https://doi.org/10.1007/978-1-4471-5358-0

Luna-Pla, I., Juárez-Gámiz;, & Julio-Vicente. (2015). *The other digital divide. The information and knowledge society. National Survey of the Information Society* . UNAM. http://www..libros.unam.mx/the-other-digital-gap-the-information-and-knowledge-society-9786070270055-book.html

Ruiz-Gutierrez, R. (2024). *Interview with Rosaura Ruiz Gutiérrez* [Interview]. UNAM. https://www.youtube.com/watch?v=DKIQ0c09mNE&t=3s

Rychen, D.S.E., & Salganik, L.H.E. (2003). *Key competencies for a successful life and a well-functioning society* . Hogrefe & Huber Publishers.

SELECT. (2022). *Home internet packages in Mexico* . SELECT. Retrieved 09/22/2024 from https://selectra.mx/internet-casa/paquetes

Slim, C. (2022). *What do we do? Carlos Slim Foundation* . Carlos Slim. Retrieved 09/22/2024 from https://fundacioncarlosslim.org/

Spiegel, J. (2021). Prensky Revisited: Is the Term "Digital Native" Still Applicable to Today's Learner? *English Leadership Quarterly* , *44* (2), 12-15.

Straubhaar, J. (2012). *Inequity in the Technopolis: Race, Class, Gender, and the Digital Divide in Austin* . University of Texas Press. https://books.google.com.mx/books?id=WQX-DAAAQBAJ

UNESCO. (2002). *Information and Communication Technology in Education: A Curriculum for Schools and Program of Teacher Development* . UNESCO. Division of higher education. https://books.google.com.mx/books?id=iOjeAQAACAAJ

UNESCO. (2005). *Towards Knowledge Societies* . UNESCO. https://books.google.com.mx/books?id=adupM6_yRPAC

Zapata-Ros, M. (2013). Assessment in the new paradigm of education in the Postindustrial Knowledge Society.

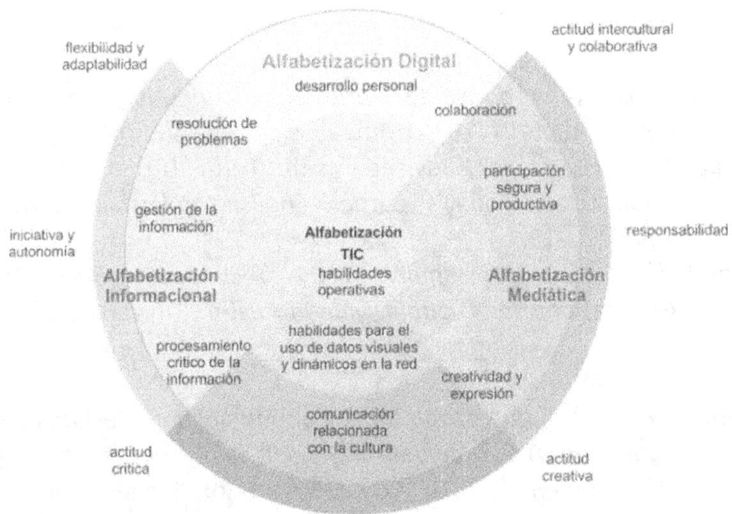

Figure 4. Literacy Model proposed by Ala Mutka in 2012.

The Digital Literacy model must be updated with the advent of recent Artificial Intelligence technologies.